ABOUT THE AUTHOR/ILLUSTRATOR

K. Michelle Edge is the author & illustrator of numerous children's titles, including her autobiographical series, "The Adventures of Sissy Dog". Michelle does her best writing in the bathtub and likes to create digital art on rainy days. The fish farmer's daughter spent her childhood in nature, growing up on the family farm in Soperton, Georgia. Swimming in the creek, hunting, fishing, climbing trees, and playing with the animals on the property were her favorite things to do. As an adult, Michelle's love for the environment and being outside quickly turned into falconry, SCUBA diving, rockhounding, sea turtle conservation, coral reef restoration, and wildlife rehabilitation. Ms. Edge has a B.S. in Natural Resources from Oregon State University and graduated Cum Laude as a first-generation college student.

WOULD YOU LIKE A SCHOOL AUTHOR VISIT?

Contact me at kmichellebooks1@gmail.com

Copyright © 2022 K. Michelle Books

All Rights Reserved.
No part of this book may be used or reproduced by any means, graphic, electronic or mechanical, including photocopying, recording, taping or by any information storage retrieval system without the written permission of the publisher except in the case of brief quotations embodied in critical articles and reviews.
Carl's Fish Farm: An Introduction to Aquaculture

www.kmichellebooks.com * kmichellebooks1@gmail.com
South Jordan, UT/Soperton, GA

Hardback ISBN: 979-8-9857366-0-1
Paperback ISBN: 978-1-63944-321-5
E-book available on Amazon Kindle
Library of Congress PCN: 9781638489092
Library of Congress Control Number: 2022931811

Carl's Fish Farm
An Introduction to Aquaculture

written & illustrated by
K. Michelle Edge

HELLO THERE!

I'm **Carl**, and today we will *see* just how fish farming started—and how it came to *be*.

Aquaculture is great! Let me tell you the *story* of how we Americans make fishy *glory*.

WE, FISH SIBLINGS, were **roe** in the pond by a *bank*. A **farmer** scooped us up and put us in a *tank*. That **hatchery** tank warmed us, so we didn't *freeze*. We could **hatch** and then **grow**, swimming just as we *please*.

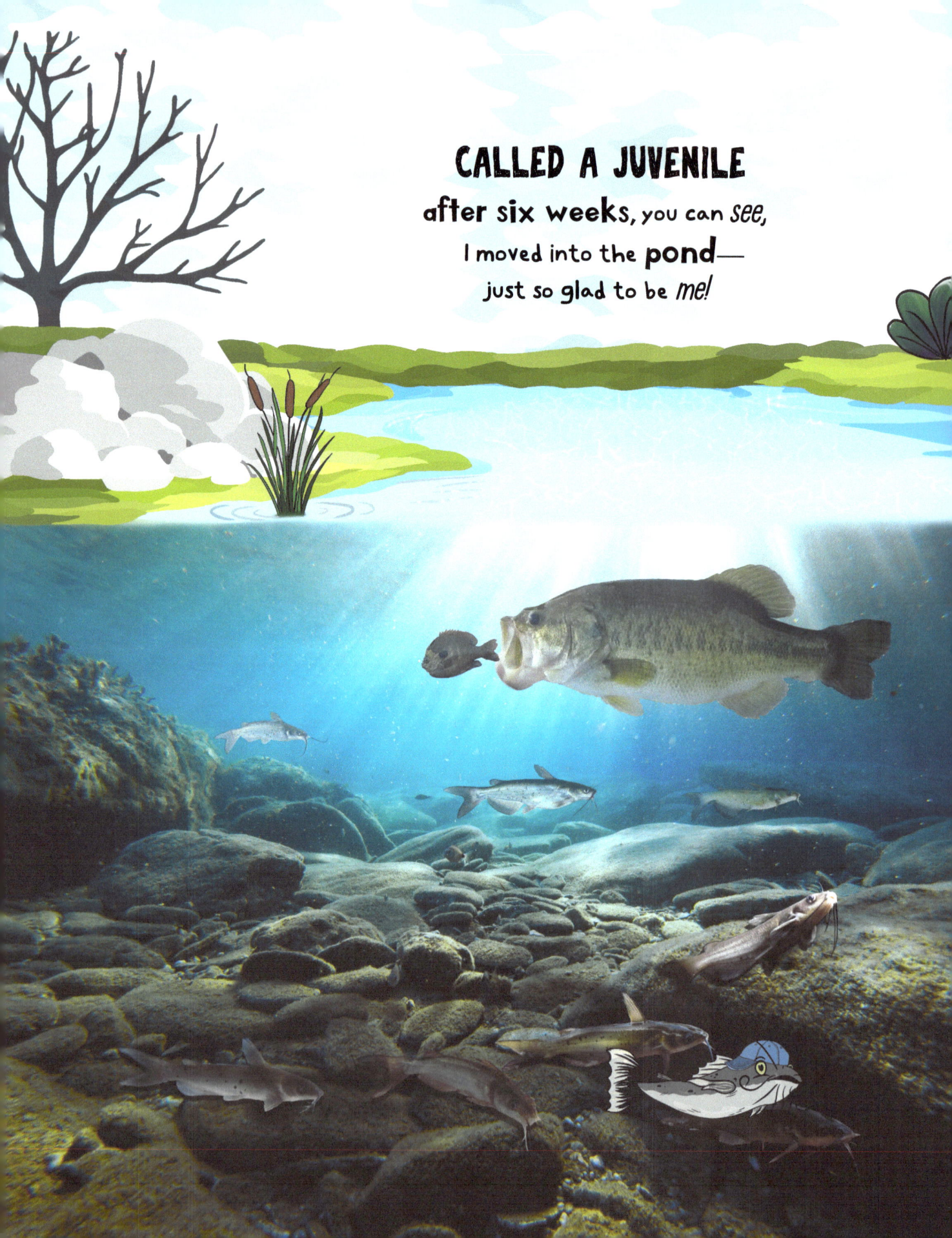

CALLED A JUVENILE

after six weeks, you can *see*,
I moved into the **pond**—
just so glad to be *me!*

WHERE TO FIND AQUACULTURE? It's here, and it's *there*.

Fish are not just in **Georgia**.
We live *everywhere!*

Average Temperature (F°)

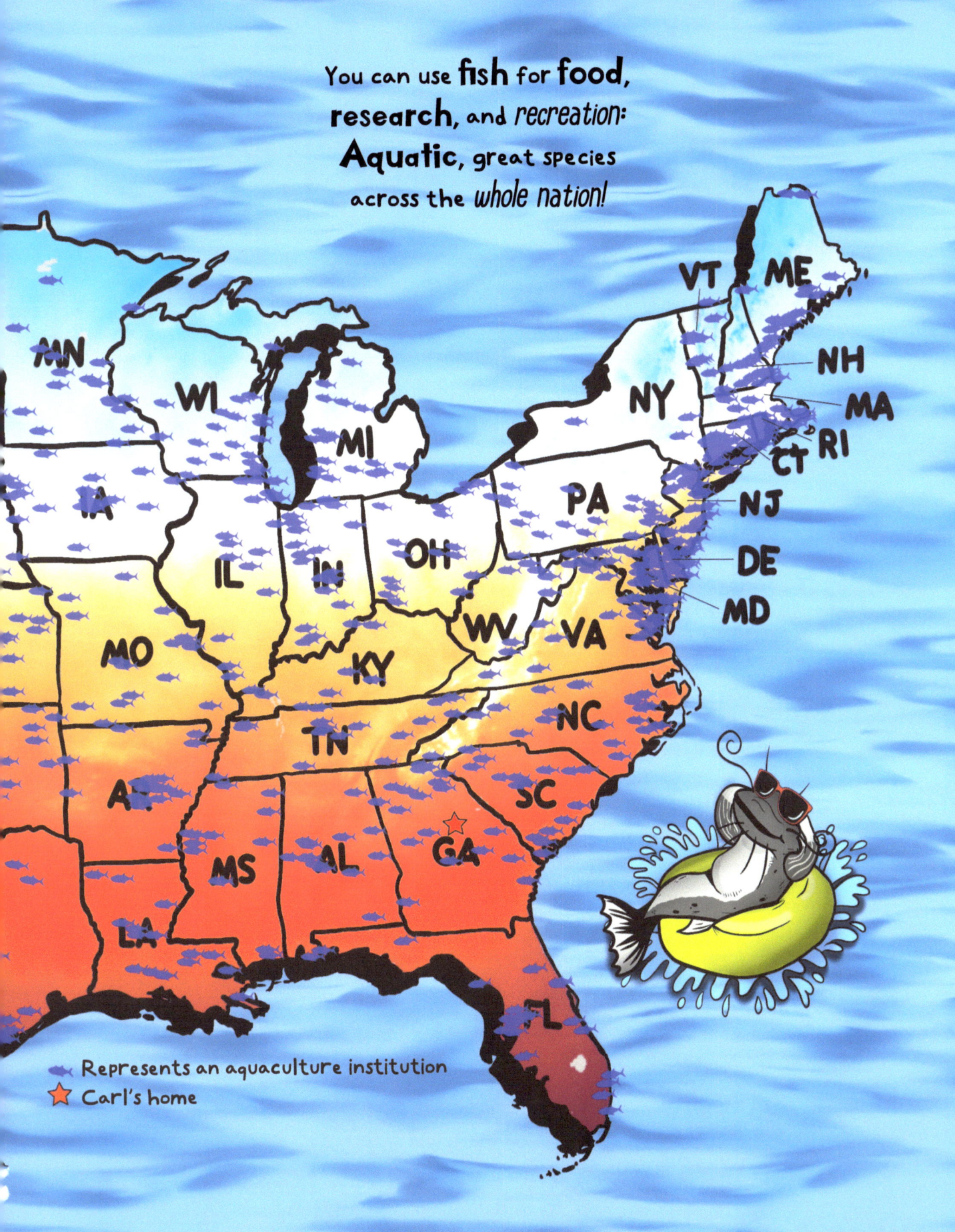

BILLY, a striped bass, is from North Dakota. The food-plant he's moving to is in Minnesota.

Now, Anna, the planktonic algae, so green—creates food, bioplastics, and fuels that are clean.

Also, Olive, the **oyster**, was born by *the sea*. She was served as **great seafood**—we all would *agree*!

Born in **streams of Alaska**, this **salmon** is *Chelsea*. She takes part in **research** on keeping fish *healthy*.

Our **enormous**, **strong net**
that we all call a *seine*,
will get **dragged** through the pond
with **two poles** made of *cane*.

FARMERS carry a seine-reel,
which keeps the net *neat*.
All controlled by a **tractor**—
a marvelous *feat!*

WE HAVE graders that sort many **fish** of all *sizes*. It **helps out** the fish when their **stress level** *rises.*

When **farmers** weigh the **fish,** they use this big *scale.*

With **minimized handling,** fish's **slime-coats** won't *fail.*

See, the farm ponds for fish are quite **different**—here's *why:*
Since they're shaped like a **rectangle**, seine nets get *by.*
Different fish need **different waters**, such as the *sea.*
Floating in round **cages**, they're on a growing *spree.*

HERE IS OUR FISH TRUCK,

which moves **fish** from **here** to *there*.
The **big tank**s full of **oxygen** bring fish fresh *air*.

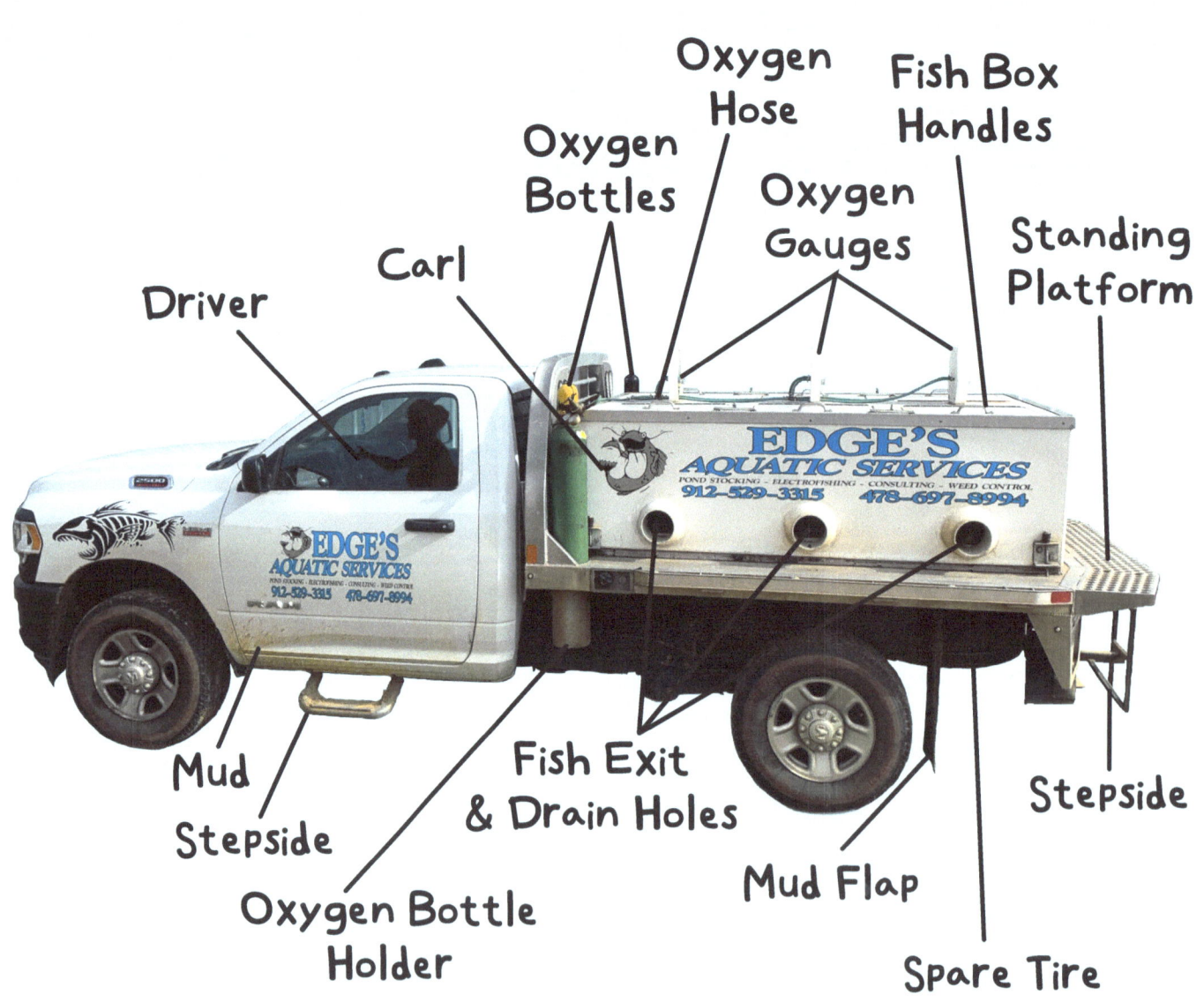

You might like **Aquaculture**—with catfish like *me*.
So, let's talk about **jobs**, there are **many**, you'll *see!*

There's a **manager, farmer,** and a **farmhand** *too*,
which are all **fishy jobs** you may want to *do*.

ICHTHYOLOGISTS, counselors, and good fish *technicians* can work **anywhere** when they fill these *positions*.

Would **you** want to be the **best** fish doctor *yet?* There are **farms** that could **certainly** use a *'fish vet'.*

Hey, is **swimming** for **you?** So then, choose scuba *diving*.

Or else you could **work** doing fish transport *driving*.

Perhaps an **instructor?**

Or a *lake engineer?*

All of these **jobs** you can **work** throughout the *year*.

THANKS FOR LEARNING with me, **Carl the Catfish**, *today.* I sure hope you like **fishing**—with good things to *say.*

So, now, **go** spread the **word**: **Aquaculture** is *fun!* Farming fish is **important.** Show folks how it's *done!*

ABOUT THE FARMERS

Kim and Keith Edge of Soperton, GA, own and operate *Edge's Aquatic Services*, a freshwater/warmwater fish hatchery that also specializes in pond and lake management for optimal trophy bass fishing. *Edge's Aquatic Services* started in a small town with big family values. **Kim** holds an A.S. in Biology from *East Georgia State College*, is a member of the *Georgia Farm Bureau Aquaculture Commodity Board*, and is on the *Southern Regional Aquaculture Center's Industry Advisory Council*. **Keith** cultivated the farm in 2000 by experimenting with raising channel catfish in cages, and he holds an herbicide applicator license from the *Georgia Department of Agriculture* for aquatic weed control. Both **Keith** and **Kim** are licensed with the *U.S. Fish & Wildlife Service* for electroshock fishing in performing aquatic ecosystem population studies. They also specialize in raising copperhead bluegill, channel catfish, largemouth bass, white perch, and many more freshwater species.

Ethan and Anna Edge own and operate *Edge's Pond Management*, the sister company to *Edge's Aquatic Services*. They provide pond management services, such as aquatic weed control, liming, high-end water quality testing, and pond fountain installation. **Ethan** holds an A.S. in Biology from *East Georgia State College*, is a board member for the *Society of Lake Management Professionals*, a member of the *Georgia Aquaculture Association*, and is a "Steward of the Water" for *SePro*, a plant management organization. **Ethan** also received his applicator license from the *Georgia Department of Agriculture* for aquatic weed control. **Anna** holds an A.A. in Business from *East Georgia State College*, is the office manager for *Edge's Pond Management*, a member of the *Georgia Aquaculture Association*, and a member of the *Society of Lake Management Professionals*. She is also a stay-at-home mom for her and Ethan's two-year-old little girl, **Maddie Rae**.

AQUACULTURE

Dr. Gary Burtle has worked in extension, teaching, and aquaculture research for 34 years at the *University of Georgia*. He has written bulletins, fact sheets, book chapters, and journal articles on aquaculture and pond management topics. Presentations to school children at First and Third Grade Field Days were a routine for **Dr. Burtle** over the past 34 years. Student Advisement, tours for school classes, aquaculture, and animal science classes at college and technical schools kept **Dr. Burtle** in touch with youth in the classroom, along with presentations to *FFA*, *4-H*, and *Boy Scouts*. **Dr. Burtle** was awarded the *Excellence in Teaching Award* in 2020 and the *Senior Extension Scientist Award* in 2007 for the *UGA College of Ag and Environmental Sciences*. In 2016, **Dr. Burtle** was recognized as a Team Leader in Catfish Marketing Demonstrations by the *Aquaculture and Fisheries Business Institute at Auburn University*.

Imani Black of Chestertown, MD, is the Founder & CEO of *Minorities In Aquaculture*, a nonprofit organization dedicated to bridging the gap between women of color and sustainable seafood through education, empowerment and career development opportunities to promote the environmental benefits provided by local and global aquaculture. Imani holds a B.S. in Marine Biology from *Old Dominion University*. Following her graduation in 2016, Imani began her aquaculture career in the *VIMS' Aquaculture Genetics & Breeding Technology Center's (ABC)*, and the *Oyster Aquaculture Training (OAT)* program, which targets those pursuing careers in all aspects of oyster aquaculture, from hatchery operations to grow-out and processing. Since then, Imani has grown her own career in both Maryland and Virginia shellfish aquaculture industries. Through her graduate research at *UMCES*, Imani is proud of her family heritage of watermen dating back over 200 years on the Eastern shore of Maryland.

HIGHLIGHTS

Bob Lusk of Texas has helped pond owners manage aquatic ecosystems for more than 40 years, and he now travels the nation as a premier consultant. Bob graduated from the *Wildlife and Fisheries Science Department* at *Texas A&M* as a fisheries biologist, and has worked for TV celebrities, *NASCAR* owners, and *John Q. Public*. Bob is also the editor of *Pond Boss Magazine*, a national bimonthly magazine dedicated to premier management of private waters. Bob often makes personal appearances at aquatic trade shows and seminars, appears on television shows and in news articles because of his vast knowledge of aquatic habitat, fish genetics, and food chains. He has also produced hundreds of YouTube videos, podcasts, articles, and radio interviews on his specialties. Bob was recently inducted into the *American Fisheries Society's esteemed Hall of Excellence*, the first fisheries biologist from the private sector to receive such an honor. He has also been awarded *the L.A. Wilke Award for Excellence* by the *Texas Outdoor Writers Association*, which is their highest and most prestigious honor.

Ozark Fisheries is a 4th generation family-owned and operated ornamental goldfish and koi farm. Since 1926, Ozark Fisheries has been raising and selling quality goldfish and koi throughout North America. Ozark Fisheries has two farm locations, with their headquarters and original farm located near Stoutland, Missouri and a second farm in Martinsville, Indiana. The Indiana farm was originally established in 1899 as *Grassyfork Fisheries* and is one of the oldest, continuously operated private fish farms in the U.S. All fish are born and raised in the U.S. and are shipped directly from the farm to your doorstep. Ozark Fisheries is a member of the *National Aquaculture Association*, as well as members of the *Missouri and Indiana Aquaculture Associations*. Ozark Fisheries is currently managed by the 3rd and 4th generations and they are looking forward to celebrating 100 years of operation in 2026.

GLOSSARY

Agriculture: Farming; cultivating soil, growing crops, or raising animals for food or other resources.

Aquaculture: Also known as fish farming, aquaculture is the raising of aquatic organisms on special farms, which can take place in open ocean, bays, ponds, greenhouses, and even in buildings. This includes seaweed, aquatic plants, algae, fish, shellfish, amphibians, alligators, turtles, crustaceans, and mollusks.

Brackish Water: Water near the ocean that is saltier than freshwater, but not as salty as the sea.

Fingerling: (30-235 days old) A baby fish whose body has developed and it about the size of a finger.

Fry: (5-30 days old) A hatchling that has shape and eats zooplankton.

Grader: A basket or device that separates fish into desired sizes.

Hatchery: A building where fish can hatch, grow, and can be processed.

Hatchling: (Just born) A freshly hatched fish that still has its yolk sac (sac fry) and is also known as larvae. The yolk sac is usually dissolved 2-3 days after hatching.

Juvenile: (235 days-2 years old) A reproductively mature fish, interacting with other adult fish.

Planktonic Algae: Microscopic plants that float in the water and produce oxygen and food. They can be used for plastics, feed, fertilizers, and much more.

Pond Stocking/Restocking: Releasing farm-raised fish into a pond, lake, or stream to balance an ecosystem or increase its population.

Roe: Fish eggs.

JOB DESCRIPTIONS

Aquatic Engineer: Someone who builds or designs ponds and dams so that they don't leak and also have an environmentally sound structure.

Farm Manager: Someone who ensures that the farm is running well.

Farmhand: Someone who performs daily work on the farm, repairs equipment, moves fish, and performs a lot of physical labor.

Fish Farmer: Someone who owns, grows, and manages a fish farm.

Fish Technician: Oversees and assists in the daily work completed at a fishery. They ensure that fish are healthy and fed.

Fish Veterinarian: A fish doctor, assessing parasites and disease. They check water quality, and make sure that aquatic animals are healthy overall.

Ichthyologist: A scientist who studies fish or any aquatic life.

Instructor: College professor for fisheries or ichthyology, tech college trainer for fish and wildlife, or high school environmental science teacher.

Policy Advisor/Counselor: Helps to create laws and regulations for aquaculture concerning national policies, ensures pond builders aren't breaking laws by destroying wetland areas. Reviews documents, and breaks down information for customers, managers, and other stakeholder organizations.

Scuba Diver: Carries out underwater welding, dock and habitat installation, counts fish, and conducts population studies. Also inspects drainpipes and installs trash catchers, performs dam assessments, and repairs boats.

Transport Driver: Obtained a CDL and transports fish from farms to ponds, food factories, or wherever they may need to go.

FREE HYDROPONICS ACTIVITY

Did you enjoy this book?

⭐⭐⭐⭐⭐

Please leave us an Amazon review!

Acknowledgements

"Agriculture Definition & Meaning." Merriam-Webster, Merriam-Webster, https://www.merriam-webster.com/dictionary/agriculture#:~:text=Kids%20Definition%20of%20agriculture,crops%2C%20and%20raising%20of%20livestock.

"Betta Fish Visits the Veterinarian." Veterinary Medicine at Illinois, https://vetmed.illinois.edu/pet-health-columns/bettat-fish-visits-vet/.

Kids Corner. National Aquaculture Association, http://thenaa.net/kids-corner.

"Nomenclature of Fish Seed." Fish Seed Rearing Manual, https://www.fao.org/3/ac381e/AC381E02.htm.

USGS - U.S. Geological Survey Water Availability and Use Science Program. "What Is 'Brackish'?" UWhat Is Brackish? - USGS National Brackish Groundwater Assessment, https://water.usgs.gov/ogw/gwrp/brackishgw/brackish.html.

Russell, Adam. "When Stocking Ponds with Fish, Stick to the Process." AgriLife Today, 12 Apr. 2021, https://agrilifetoday.tamu.edu/2020/04/08/when-stocking-ponds-with-fish-stick-to-the-process/.

"The History of Aquaculture." Alimentarium, https://www.alimentarium.org/en/knowledge/history-aquaculture#:~:text=The%20earliest%20evidence%20of%20fish,as%20being%20farmed%20for%20food.

Southern Regional Aquaculture Center, College Station, Texas, 1991, pp. 1-4, Water Quantity and Quality Requirements for Channel Catfish Hatcheries. Lindsey, Rebecca. "New Maps of Annual Average Temperature and Precipitation from the U.S. Climate Normals." New Maps of Annual Average Temperature and Precipitation from the U.S. Climate Normals | NOAA Climate.gov, https://www.climate.gov/news-features/featured-images/new-maps-annual-average-temperature-and-precipitation-us-climate. (Information for temperature map on page 11/12 provided by NOAA)

"Planktonic Algae - Aquaplant: Management of Pond Plants & Algae." AquaPlant, 3 Dec. 2020, https://aquaplant.tamu.edu/plant-identification/alphabetical-index/planktonic-algae/#:~:text=Planktonic%20algae%20blooms%20are%20considered,areas%20over%202%20feet%20deep).

Fisheries, NOAA. "Sugar Kelp." NOAA, https://www.fisheries.noaa.gov/species/sugar-kelp.

"Fishery Policy Analyst, ZP-0401-3/4 (DE/CR)." American Geosciences Institute, 23 Mar. 2020, https://www.americangeosciences.org/workforce/jobs/fishery-policy-analyst-zp-0401-34-decr#:~:text=Advises%20management%20on%20the%20development,materials%20related%20to%20aquaculture%20management.

"Florida Alligator Meat, Skins and Hides." Florida Alligator Meat, Skins and Hides / Buy "Fresh From Florida" / Consumer Resources / Home - Florida Department of Agriculture & Consumer Services, https://www.fdacs.gov/Consumer-Resources/Buy-Fresh-From-Florida/Florida-Alligator-Meat-Skins-and-Hides. https://www.clemson.edu/extension/water/stormwater-ponds/problem-solving/aquatic-weeds/algae-planktonic/index.html#:~:text=Planktonic%20algae%20are%20microscopic%20plants,every%20drop%20of%20pond%20water.&text=These%20tiny%20plants%20get%20their,i.e.%20fertilizer)%20in%20the%20water.

PHOTOS

Photos on pages 7, 15, & 20, provided & licensed by Shutterstock (enhanced/commercial license purchased by author).

Photos on pages 3, 4, 9, 14, 16, 17, provided & licensed by Unsplash (enhanced/commercial license not required). Photos taken by Amber Kipp, John Angel, Milo Weiler, Yannis Panpastasopoulos, & Edrin Spahiu.

Photos on pages 5, 8, 10, 13, 18, 19, 21, 22, 23, 24, & 29 donated by Edge's Aquatic Services and Edge's Pond Management

Photos & biographies for Aquaculture Highlights donated by Bob Lusk, Dr. Gary Burtle & Ozark Fisheries. (Page 28)

A special thank-you to **Lauren Goble**, **Kim Edge**, and **Kim Thompson** for their insight, to **Robin Katz OTD** for her metered editing skills, to **Jess Croft**, **April Hamm**, **Khairah Green**, and **Lor Bingham** for their proofreading and critique, to **Ryan Webb** for his cover design, to **Imani Black**, **Dr. Gary Burtle**, **Bob Lusk**, and **Ozark Fisheries** for sharing their roles in Aquaculture, and to **Kim and Keith** at **Edge's Aquatic Services** and **Ethan, Anna, and Maddie Rae** at **Edge's Pond Management** for allowing their farm and their lives to be shared in this book.

It wouldn't have been possible without you! ~Michelle